The Sea Lions of Los Islotes

The Jewel of Espíritu Santo Island

Luke Inman

2nd Edition

ISBN 978-1-909455-49-8

Second edition

A catalogue record for this book can be
obtained from the British Library.

Published 2022 by

DIVED UP

Dived Up Publications
Oxford • United Kingdom
Email info@divedup.com
www.DivedUp.com

"Some people talk to animals. Not many listen though. That's the problem."

—Winnie the Pooh, A A Milne

The Sea Lions of Los Islotes

CONTENTS

Foreword

Luke Inman and I have worked together many times over the years, yielding some of my fondest wildlife memories. We've trekked through the deserts of Baja, catching all the local species of rattlesnake, and lain in the dust alongside a thumb-sized tarantula hawk wasp doing battle with a giant spider trying to lock it in a lethal embrace. Many of my finest moments though have been in the Sea of Cortez. This is quite simply one of the finest bodies of water on the planet for experiencing natural wonders. From freediving down into inky blue depths, and enjoying a twirling twisting submarine duet with a female California sea lion, to finning in plankton-rich green alongside leviathan whale sharks. From tussling with mighty Humboldt squid, the lurid alien spaceships of the deep, to struggling to keep pace with a diving sperm whale. All these glories have been made possible by Luke, his enthusiasm, knowledge, and passion for the part of the world he has made home.

Steve Backshall

Steve is a BAFTA-winning English naturalist, writer and television presenter.

The Sea Lions of Los Islotes

Introduction

Arriving at the sea lion colony of Los Islotes, visitors are heralded by an auditory overload. Instead of trumpets, you are surrounded by a cacophony of barks, the ringing cries of sea birds, the slap of waves against the boat's hull, and the rumble of the ocean swell over the rocky embankment. All this is punctuated by sea lion howls and whines.

The sea lions noisily hail each other and the boats—welcoming visitors to their world. The constant hubbub penetrates your soul, driving home the message that "magic happens here." You cannot help but be enchanted by these creatures. They emanate finesse and charm without a hint of illusion or wizardry. There is no incantation or voodoo, just an abounding sense of play that inspires every visitor.

When it comes to wild animal encounters, Los Islotes is almost *nirvana*. Few places so close to a city can truly offer such a convenient and accessible opportunity to interact with Mother Nature in her untamed state. Initial introductions begin at the surface; encounters are then formalized below the water as Poseidon's ocean ambassadors exuberantly whiz towards and around diver and snorkeler alike. Their welcoming salutations are conducted face-to-face, no pens or exhibit walls can be found here.

Sea lions taught me that serenity could be found in wild animal interactions. Their doctrine is euphoric, their lives utopic, leaving you smiling and remembering your own childhood innocence and the joy found in those halcyon, care-free days.

I created this project to try and demonstrate the importance of us making stronger connections with wild animals and hopefully fostering a greater sense of conservation.

The sea lions have provided some of my most incredible wild animal encounters. Hopefully I have captured their spirit and a sense of their unforgettable home within these pages.

If this book inspires you to seek out your own wild animal encounter and savor the spiritual connection it engenders, then I will consider it a success.

LOS ISLOTES
ESPÍRITU SANTO ISLAND

"When someone evokes Los Islotes at Espíritu Santo Island, images of crystal clear water come to mind. A rocky reef filled with incredible biodiversity and inhabited by a colony of friendly sea lions that one may swim with.

Espíritu Santo Island and Los Islotes are recognized worldwide for their incomparable scenic beauty, as well as the well-developed level of conservation that makes them unique. Together they belong to the Biosphere Reserve known as Area Natural Protegida de Islas del Golfo de California (Natural Protected Area of the Islands of the Gulf of California) which was declared a UNESCO Natural World Heritage site in 2005.

The sea lion colony at Los Islotes is more than a tourist attraction, it is the southernmost breeding colony in the Gulf of California, with healthy and stable conditions and over 500 specimens recorded to date. It is regularly monitored with assistance from the tourist industry.

Los Islotes physically resembles a cathedral that could have been thought up by a vanguardist architect such as Gaudi. It is composed of a series of cliffs and rocky promontories, as well as an archway through which one may traverse the natural structure, crowned by the guano of the birds which gather there to feed on the abundant sea life, or nest there due to the safety it provides.

There is no doubt that Los Islotes is a place worthy of being visited and admired, which is why this collection of images that pay it homage brings us closer to the natural splendor found therein."

Irma González López

Director of the Protected Natural Area of the Gulf of California Islands in the state of Baja California Sur and of the Espíritu Santo Archipelago Marine Park.

LOS ISLOTES

Sea of Cortez

BAJA
CALIFORNIA
SUR

ISLA Espíritu SANTO

Pacific Ocean

N

The Sea Lions of Los Islotes

The Islets

Los Islotes is located just north of Isla Partida and Espíritu Santo in the Espíritu Santo Archipelago. "Los Islotes" means "the islets" in Spanish and never has a place so suited its name. At low tide it is a single islet, whereas at high tide it is two.

Los Islotes looms out of the ocean with an austere and rugged appearance. Rich evidence of Baja's geologic history can be found in the starkly weathered volcanic rock formations. The islet is pockmarked with grottos, caves, and a freestanding arch at its eastern end that allows divers and snorkelers to swim from one side to the other.

Below the surface swirl thousands of different species of marine animals in a kaleidoscope of color and motion. Small delicate cup corals and soft gorgonians cling to the rocks while Cortez angelfish and large schools of yellow surgeonfish glide overhead.

Los Islotes' main inhabitants are California sea lions (*Zalophus californianus*). This is their southernmost home in a habitat ranging along the Pacific coast. The colony's population increased from 200 to 400 in 2005 and has remained stable in the years following, strangely thriving in a location that receives more tourists than other islands in the Sea of Cortez. This is a bit of a paradox when you consider the fact their numbers are declining in other parts of the sea also known as the Gulf of California.

Since 1995, Mexican law has classified the archipelago as a Marine Protected Area.

The Sea Lions of Los Islotes

The Sea Lions of Los Islotes

Three Different Areas

ZONE B

ZONE C

ZONE A

Researchers[1] have divided Los Islotes into three main zones: A, B and C. Zones A and B are the main reproductive areas, while Zone C was historically a "bachelor" area, occupied by single males either too young or too old to reproduce. As numbers increase, the bachelor area decreases in size and portions of zone C become repurposed for breeding.

Los Islotes receives more tourists than any other attraction in La Paz or the archipelago. It is the responsibility of everyone to ensure both visitors and sea lions stay safe and free from harassment. Failure to observe the guidelines could lead to panic, altered behavior, and even an animal stampede that could result in sudden death of precious and vulnerable sea lion pups.

These creatures are insatiably inquisitive and playful, yet they are still wild and need to be respected. The Mexican government has laid down some basic rules to ensure a safe and memorable encounter. I can testify to having never had an aggressive experience during my many interactions with these joyous beasts.

Why? I strictly follow the rules.

---

1   At Centro Interdisciplinario de Ciencias Marinas (CICIMAR), including Dr Fernando Elorriaga.

The Sea Lions of Los Islotes

The Rules of Los Islotes

- Do not disembark on the island or stand on the rocks.

- Be passive when swimming with the sea lions, let them approach you.

- Avoid making loud sounds (using speakers, boat klaxons, or releasing air from scuba tanks).

- Report the presence of any entangled or wounded sea lions to the authorities.

- Photographers and videographers should not harass the sea lions in an attempt to get a better photo or video.

- Boats should anchor using the buoys provided or at least 30 m (90 ft) from the island.

- When swimming with the sea lions, do not approach closer than 5 m (15 ft) to the main rookery area (zones A and B).

"It seems to me that the natural world is the greatest source of excitement; the greatest source of visual beauty; the greatest source of intellectual interest. It is the greatest source of so much in life that makes life worth living."

—Sir David Attenborough

Water touches everything

Whether you plunge into the
ocean, swim across a lake, ford
a river, or touch a glacier, you
are developing the connection.
Water is all encompassing.
The vast Atlantic may once
have been part of the Pacific,
the tributaries of the Amazon or
the glaciers of Patagonia. This
association and relationship
with the ocean has become an
essential part of my life. The sea
lions are my meditation—visiting
and associating with them has
become a key component of
my routine, a natural, nurturing
therapy.

Los Islotes

SEA LIONS

What's in a Name?

Sea lions are members of the group called pinnipeds (Latin for fin-feet). They can be differentiated from seals by the presence of small ears, a sharper nose, and the ability to walk using their four extremities, which makes them more "terrestrial" than their seal cousins. This difference also relates to their diving ability. Sea lions can only hold their breath for a maximum of 20 minutes, while seals can stay submerged for up to an hour.

Mexico is home to four different species of pinnipeds: the harbor seal; Northern elephant seal; Guadalupe fur seal; and the California sea lion—the last of these being the only permanent resident in the Sea of Cortez. The population totals about 25,000 individuals throughout the region.

The California sea lion inhabits waters from Vancouver Island in Canada to the southern Sea of Cortez.

You are probably most familiar with the role of these animals as a major draw in marine attractions around the world. They are often seen balancing beach balls and jumping through hoops in exchange for a fishy inducement. These performances may leave a lasting impression on the audience, but the animals pay a heavy price. Marine mammals in particular should not be kept in captivity as they suffer health problems and perish earlier than wild animals.

It is infinitely preferable to encounter these creatures in the wild where you can appreciate their graceful, playful and intelligent nature. Instead of observing marine mammals confined to prison—in tanks of glass or steel—visitors to Los Islotes are rewarded with sightings and memorable interactions with exuberant animals socialising and thriving in the wild.

Sea Lions

The California sea lion has an elongated and slender body, a blunt snout, and a distinctly shorter tail than other pinnipeds. Adult males grow considerably larger than adult females and have a noticeably raised forehead ridge.

The fore flippers are long and show distinct claws.
Sea lions are also notoriously noisy, with males having
loud territorial barks while females wail and growl.

Californian sea lions have the longest and most sensitive whiskers of any mammal—they can detect textures and shapes to the same sensitivity as human fingertips, in water so cold fingers would go numb.

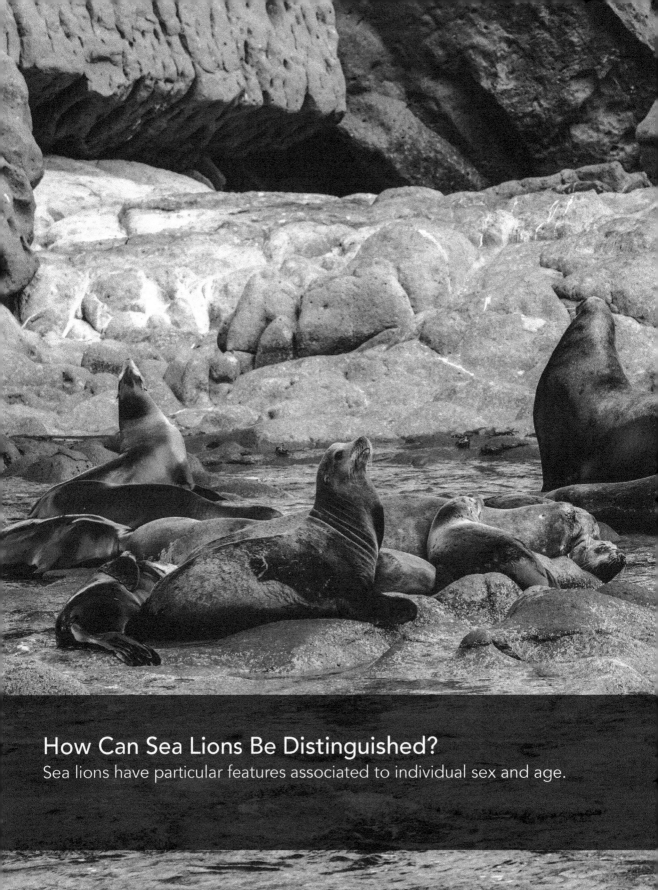

How Can Sea Lions Be Distinguished?
Sea lions have particular features associated to individual sex and age.

The Sea Lions of Los Islotes

ADULT MALES

Individuals are considered adult males when they are older than nine years. They have a dark brown color and reach 2–2.5 m (6.5–8.25 ft) long, weighing up to 500 kg (1100 lbs). These males have a broad neck and a prominent sagittal crest, expressed as an obvious protuberance of the head, unique in this species.

The Sea Lions of Los Islotes

Adult Males

SUB-ADULT MALES

Sub-adult males are between five and eight years old and they have similar coloring to full adult males. They measure 1.5–2.3 m (5–7.5 ft) in length and weigh approximately 200 kg (440 lbs). Their neck and sagittal crest are not so prominent, compared to adult males. Many members of this category can be seen in Los Islotes between November and March due to a winter migration related to feeding. It is thought that these animals come from rookeries in the central Gulf of California.

Sub-Adult Males

The Sea Lions of Los Islotes

Sub-Adult Males

The Sea Lions of Los Islotes

ADULT FEMALES

Adult females are five years and older. They have a light brown color and reach 1.4–1.9 m (4.6–6.2 ft) in length. They have an approximated weight of 100 kg (220 lbs). Females do not have a sagittal crest or the broad neck of males.

Adult females are the most abundant of all the categories and are also found with the highest typical life span (20–25 years) in a sea lion population. This is because they have a less hazardous lifestyle, do not engage in physical competition and are not so obligated by natural selection to grow as the males, whose average life span is only 15–17 years.

Adult Females

JUVENILES

The juveniles are between one and four years old. They measure 1–1.3 m (3.3–4.25 ft) in length and are not physically/sexually mature. At this age it is not possible to distinguish a male from a female. Although lactation ceases at the end of the first year, it is possible to see two- or three-year-old juveniles feeding from their mothers, something not so common in other sea lion or seal species.

Juveniles

The Sea Lions of Los Islotes

Juveniles

The Sea Lions of Los Islotes

Juveniles

The Sea Lions of Los Islotes

PUPS

Pups are animals of both sexes under one year old. They are dark grey or black in color. Most births in the Gulf of California occur between the end of May and the end of July. At birth, females measure on average 75 cm (2.5 ft) and weigh 6.5 kg (14 lbs). Newborn males tend to weigh 1 kg (2.2 lbs) more. Although lactation lasts one year, pups start feeding on fish and crustaceans at eight months old. From that time up to their first birthday many pups die because their life is increasingly spent at sea, making them more vulnerable to predators, illness and accidents.

The Sea Lions of Los Islotes

Pups

" *The supreme good is like water, which nourishes all things without trying to. It is content with the low places that people disdain. Thus it is like the Thao.* **"**

—Lao Tzu

FEEDING

The Sea Lions of Los Islotes

The Search for Food

Sea lions live off over 100 different species of fish as well as some species of squid. The inhabitants of Los Islotes feed predominately on deep-sea species, hunting in groups to corner their prey. Hunting is carried out mainly at night or near dawn when deeper-dwelling fish and squid ascend to the surface to feed, where they are increasingly vulnerable to the sea lions.

Their hunting grounds tend to be close to shore. Recent studies using satellite tracking of the sea lions at Los Islotes have shown the animals can, on average, travel 30 km (18 miles) in search of prey. More astonishingly, male sea lions have been known to travel hundreds of kilometers during migrations.

Scientists at CICIMAR have found evidence that the sea lions at Los Islotes are hunting fish deeper than animals from other colonies in the Gulf of California. This is believed to be a key factor in the success of this colony, despite it receiving more tourist visitors than any of the others.

REPRODUCTION
AND NURSING

Timing is Everything

The breeding season at Los Islotes starts at the end of May when the females give birth. Approximately 28 days later the females will mate again.

Mothers give birth to one pup each year after an eleven month gestation. The fecundated ovule remains latent for two months—in a process known as delayed implantation—before nine months of development. This ensures the pups are born during the same season every year. Once pups are born, mothers fast for about four to five days to prepare to intensively feed them. This also bonds pup to mother, enabling them to recognize each other when females return from hunting trips. Lactation can last at least one year.

Sea lions are polygenic, meaning reproductive groups are made up of a single adult male and a group of females known as a harem. Males protect their territories from other males and establish dominance by vocalizing and sometimes fighting on land or in the water. Males can be fiercely aggressive during the breeding season due to this strong competition.

The Sea Lions of Los Islotes

INTERACTIONS WITH SEA LIONS

An Education

Los Islotes receives more visitors than almost any other island in the Sea of Cortez. The sea lions appear to have become accustomed to human interaction and high levels of boat traffic with few ill effects. It would be impossible to write about every one of my own interactions, but they have been universally delightful—even when they involve the menacingly large adult males.

Los Islotes is regularly featured in the diving press as one of the top ten dive sites in the world. From my perspective and experience, and I have been fortunate to have dived all over the world, Los Islotes is my number one. Most people would expect me to pick a deep wreck, an abundant pelagic site or a mystical *cenote* as my favorite, but no—a shallow dive with an uninhibited sea lion at Los Islotes will always be first choice.

One of my most memorable experiences with a young pup came with a yearling female, marked and tagged coincidentally with the number "42". She seemed to appear every time I dived at Los Islotes and taught me a lot about consorting with sea lions. She was patient, kind, and above all affectionate. Whether she really held the answer to "life, the universe and everything," is a matter of debate, but I am sure that Ford Prefect and Arthur Dent would have agreed with me. Perhaps like her dolphin cousins she was just thanking me for all the fish because soon after Los Islotes would make way for a new hyperspace bypass…who knows?

Our interactions always started with her gently colliding with me—but perhaps ambushing would be a better description. This act executed with the skill of a well-trained military diver. Like all good surprise attacks I was invariably completely blindsided, but invariably and without exception she ended with her head pressed against mine so that I could feel her whiskers caressing my forehead. She would then initiate play by gently biting my hand. This teasing nip would be the transition that ensured my hand was directed either across her body or behind her ear.

Interactions with Sea Lions

The Sea Lions of Los Islotes

When you encounter the curious playfulness of a California sea lion, the enchantment of water escalates. I have had the greatest privilege to travel all across the planet and experience some of Mother Nature's most breathtaking sights and creations. One spot alone stopped me in my tracks, so much it inspired me to set down roots. That place is Los Islotes.

Memory

Her goal seemed to be to get me to scratch her ears—when I stopped she would maneuver her head under my hand, initiating more tactile affection like dogs and puppies do. At times I would have to put my camera down and simply focus on giving her the love and attention she insisted on.

At some point 42 stopped appearing on my dives. I assumed that she had become too old or mature to continue to play with this bubbly, noisy intruder into her world. How wrong I was. Two or three years later, a by then large female greeted me underwater like a long-lost friend.

I had never witnessed profuse exuberance quite like this. It didn't seem possible that this might be the same young pup that had so gleefully sought my company. The ambush technique seemed very familiar, as did the insistence on ear and tummy rubs. Once again I found myself putting down my camera and appeasing my long-lost friend's request for some bonding and playtime.

There was scarring from an identification tag, but the actual tag had long since worn away. I asked one of the regular researchers at the colony if it was credible for 42 to remember me. I was given a suitably skeptical look and told, "There is no reason why not, but we don't look for things like that in science."

The Sea Lions of Los Islotes

PLAYTIME

Curiosity

Sea lions as well as whales, dolphins and other mammals, show a curious inclination towards exploration and play. This is most prevalent in pups and juvenile animals. On some occasions they can be seen biting divers' fins or other unfamiliar objects. Juveniles have even been seen biting big whale shark fins and chasing diving sea birds underwater. All of this behavior is without a doubt related to learning and environment recognition.

*Like labradors with tennis balls,
the sea lions play with the starfish*

The Sea Lions of Los Islotes

The Sea Lions of Los Islotes

OTHER VISITORS

*A diver backs off from an approaching whale shark to ensure
the world's largest fish fits into the viewfinder of her camera.*

Mobula ray migration takes place all along the Baja Sur peninsula. The best months to spot them around Espíritu Santo island are May and June.

The archipelago is home to an immensely diverse number of creatures. Some of them seasonally migrate through the area, but many call Isla Espíritu Santo home regardless of their range. They are a delight to tourist and local alike.

Every photograph in this book was taken within a 500 m (1,600 ft) radius of the Los Islotes sea lion colony.

WHAT CHALLENGES DO THEY FACE?

Losing the Game

The main problem that these sea lions face is safe access to food sources. During their hunting trips, they encounter abandoned or lost fishing nets and inevitably there are those who get caught in them. Some of these victim animals drown. A few luckier ones escape, taking fragments of nets with them, often tangled around their neck, causing wounds, infection or strangulation as the animal grows or time elapses.

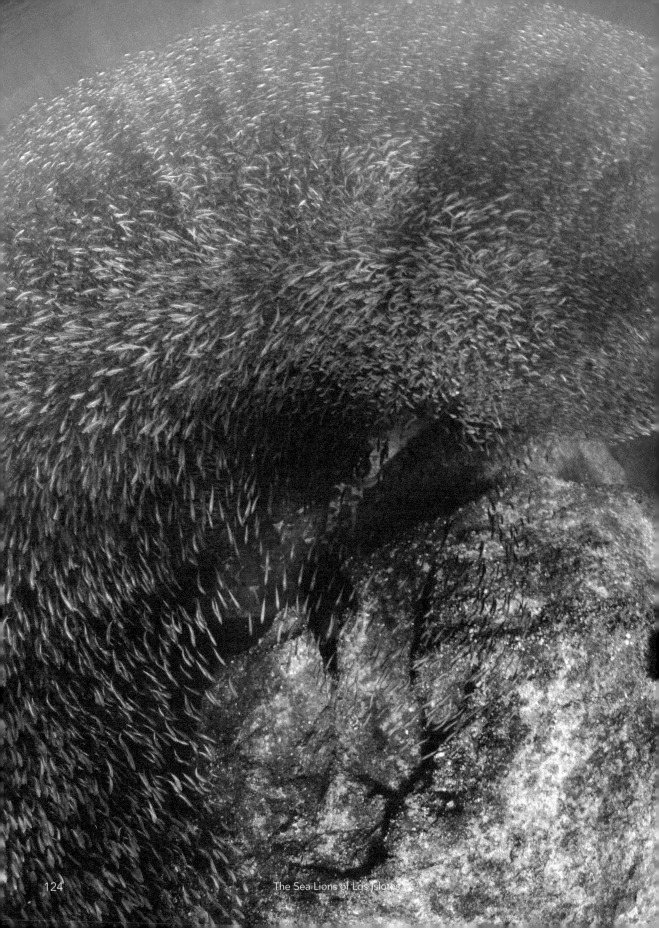

The Sea Lions of Los Islotes

The future of Los Islotes depends on many factors. I deeply wish I could do something about them all. The combined challenge presented by climate change, increases in predation and reduction in food sources is way beyond any individual's control.

The Espíritu Santo Marine Zone National Park will always provide a refuge for the sea lions and the Mexican park rangers will always do their best with the resources and tools that the government provides them with.

One essential component is the ethics and professionalism of tourism companies, the visitors and how they choose to interact with the sea lions. As the volume of tourists coming to see the colony grows, the responsibilities of those visitors and the charter boats they travel on heighten.

Los Islotes is truly a magical place—it is one of my favorite places on Earth. My wishes and desires are that it remains that way.

The Sea Lions of Los Islotes

How to Photograph a Sea Lion

Sea lions are quick, very quick. They move like lighting and are rambunctious when they want attention, aloof when feeling impersonal and unwavering when play and interaction are on their agenda. Above all they are photogenic, gracious, inquisitive supermodels of the underwater world.

It does not matter if you are scuba diving or snorkeling, using a state-of-the-art mirrorless camera in an expensive housing or a basic plastic protector for a mobile/cell phone. I have photographed sea lions using Nikonos V cameras with film, HDV video, IMAX, 4K, 6K, mirrorless and everything in between. These are my suggestions for getting good images.

Be ready and respect the environment by having perfect dive skills and buoyancy. Do not harass the sea lions, let them come to you. Like all natural history interactions, be patient.

Try the following: set a shutter speed of 250–320, use shutter priority to reduce your variables and focus on strobe position and composition. Aperture f7–f8 and ISO 320. Point your camera up and stay shallow—no deeper than 8–10m (25–30ft). Use the widest lens you have—the wider the lens, especially a fisheye, the more forgiving it is going to be.

Try not to shoot continuously. I find "single shot" far more reliable for good lighting with sea lions. Put strobes in their lowest setting to give just a "kiss" of light. Recycle time will improve, enabling you to capture more of these fast-moving subjects.

A perfect example of what it can be like to photograph sea lions is the time I took my good friend Cristina Zenato to Los Islotes. Cristina's work in ocean conservation, exploration and education with wild animals, especially sharks, has earned her the rightful recognition of The Women Divers Hall of Fame, The Explorers Club, the Ocean Artists Society and all the scuba diving agencies.

The setting was perfect, with amazing visibility and calm seas. Cristina is one of the most experienced divers in the world. So photographing her was going to be easy...or so we thought.

The sea lions came zooming in, perhaps intrigued by the calmness a diver like Cristina exudes. We tried to photograph for a good hour and came away with just one usable image. The sea lion that befriended Cristina only sat in one place...right on top of her head. No playing, not anything, just sitting on her head! No amount of coaching, coaxing or cajoling would stop this young individual from being her hat! Sometimes sea lions just don't want to cooperate.

The Sea Lions of Los Islotes

How to Photograph a Sea Lion

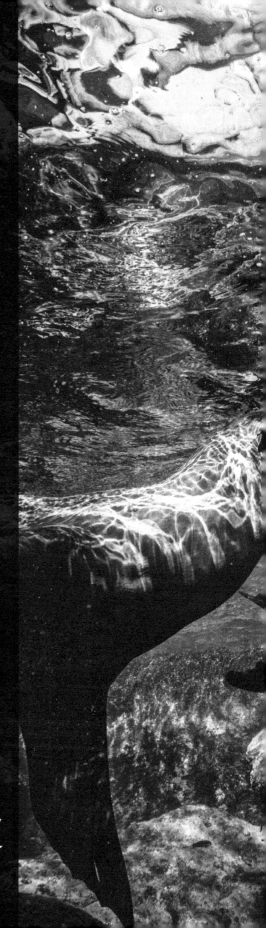

Special Thanks

It is not easy to sit down and write a special thank you to everyone who has helped and influenced this work, purely for fear of leaving somebody out.

Immediate thanks go to my mother and grandmother for instilling in me a respect and compassion for nature. To my father, for putting up with all my nonsense, and my stepmother and Chad Koll for editing my terrible dyslexic prose. To the rest of my immediate family for not being too upset about the fact I never manage to attend family functions because I am on the other side of the planet—invariably underwater—and embracing my absence with nothing but love and care when I finally appear, jet-lagged and incoherent at Heathrow Airport.

Luke Inman

This book was created using the following equipment:

fourth element

Additional Credits
Photo Editing: Maru Tzia
Aerial Photography: Aleph Alighieri
Editors: Chad H Koll, Veronica Inman
    and Alex Gibson
Scientific Editing: Fernando Elorriaga
Editorial Design: Maru Tzia
Sea Lion Illustration: Jessica Taylor
Illustrations: Carlos Juvera and
    Christian Aviles

About the Author

Luke Inman is an award-winning scuba Instructor Trainer, natural history filmmaker, photographer, writer, explorer and dog walker. He has shot underwater for various channels, publications, commissions, editorials and advertising campaigns, including the BBC's *Planet Earth 3*, Netflix's *Our Planet* and many for Fourth Element.

Luke holds the highest possible recreational and technical qualifications with PADI and his participation on various expeditions, including scientific work and diving to 118 m (398 ft) in the Sea of Cortez earned him a Fellowship of The Explorers Club in New York.

Luke is also the Owner and Operator of The Dive Gurus—the only PADI 5 Star Instructor Development Centre in La Paz, Baja California Sur, Mexico. In 2022 he was invited to become a judge and underwater expert for the Comedy Wildlife Awards.

As a committed ocean advocate, it is Luke's belief that through scuba diving we can encourage people to learn about the marine world and have more sustainable, positive interactions with wild animals that will lead to nurturing and conserving the oceans.

Lightning Source UK Ltd.
Milton Keynes UK
UKHW051234271022
411137UK00005B/35